Old Family Photos

by
G. B. Blakeslee

Copyright © 2011 by G. B. Blakeslee
Portions reproduced under Creative Commons license.

All rights reserved. No part of this book may be reproduced in any form or by electronic or mechanical means, including information storage and retrieval systems, without permission from the publisher, except by a reviewer who may quote brief passages in a review.

The characters and events in this book are fictitious. Any resemblance to real persons, either living or dead, is coincidental and not intended by the author. All photographs in this book were sourced from public domain and Creative Comons resources and, according to the publishers research, clear of copyright protection or restrictions. Any inquiries may be directed to the publisher.

ISBN-13: 978-0615567044 (Center Of Gravity)
ISBN-10: 0615567045

Publish November 2011

This work dedicated to my mother, Carl Janiece Dagnell.
Thank you to Julie Rain and many others for encouraging this work,
and my endless appreciation to Carol Reid for editorial and design assistance.

Published by

Center Of Gravity
PO Box 422
Upland, CA 91785

Twice-removed great great uncle Lyman Lee Hillford and his wife Constance were very proud of their three beautiful children — Abigail, Granville and Lyman Junior. However, the three children were plagued by nightmares and tragically disappeared shortly after this photo was taken.

As a youngster, thrice-removed fourth cousin Lysetta Elle Burkham was overjoyed to meet John Wayne, until she discovered that he, too, was stuffed.

My twice-removed fifth cousin Peter Clayton Englehardt grew up on his parent's ostrich farm, and found every possible means to promote the ostrich for its usefulness. In the late 1920's he set out to ride this ostrich, Herman, across the US on a promotional trip. Tragically, he ran out of funds halfway across, somewhere near the present-day town of Clinton, Oklahoma, and was forced to shoot his beloved Herman. When asked about the incident later all he would say was "Tastes like chicken."

This is third cousin four-times-removed Orville "Simon" Spracht. He was born in New York City and traveled all over the US, and all over the world. Still, we don't talk about him much.

The man in the picture is twice-removed great uncle Thomas Horn Cornby. He was a very successful salesman, and won many awards and bonuses from the company he worked for, Phillip Morris. Way to go, Great Uncle Thomas!

Thrice-removed third cousin Annie Cole Amberton, right, won world-wide fame as an organ-grinder. She was invited to perform at the World's Columbian Exposition held in Chicago in 1893 (also known as the Chicago World Fair.) Unfortunately, when traveling to the Exposition she was forced to check her monkey Franklin into baggage and he was incorrectly transferred to Schenectady, New York, where he founded and ran a successful ice cream parlor until his death in 1911. To the left of Annie is her husband, Joe.

Ninth-removed great uncle Maxwell Ernst Ploughman and his wife Ermina pose with their family pet and alligator, Po-Bo, found orphaned during a trip to the Great Okefenokee Swamp in southeast Georgia. Childless, the couple lavished attention on Po-Bo, taking him on all subsequent trips and dressing him in the latest fashions. When, miraculously, their first daughter was born they still considered Po-Bo part of the family.

Little Lilly, first daughter of ninth-removed great uncle Maxwell Ernst Ploughman and his wife Ermina, poses with the family pet and alligator, Po-Bo. Po-Bo, considered a wild and dangerous animal by some and a ceaseless reptile by others, was treated as a member of the family and fed specially-prepared chicken gizzards and lambs feet as treats.

Little Leander, seventh child of ninth-removed great uncle Maxwell Ernst Ploughman and his wife Ermina, was born too late to enjoy the family's recently deceased family pet and alligator, Po-Bo. However, every effort was made to continue the family tradition of photos with Po-Bo.

Twin brothers and sixth cousins twice removed, Oscar "Sleet" and Gilbert "Pine" Smith were early contestants in the lost sport of wilderness boxing. Competing in adverse conditions across forest-y swaths of primeval Ohio, fighters could use any weapons and any means to overcome their opponent, including dead boughs, spiny pinecones, and the occasional hapless raccoon. Here they are shown at the height of their careers, shortly before the unfortunate "Badger Incident."

Pictured here are twice-removed sixth cousins Albert Tiburon Rathaway, left, and his brothers Joel Obediah Rathaway and Rudolph Thaddeus Rathaway. We only point out Albert because he was so tall, so incredibly tall.

Percy McKinley Corbin, five-times-removed fifth cousin, was a savant accepted into the Colonel Sanders Cordon Bleu Institute in Carmi, Kentucky at the age of four. It's rumored that he provided the seventh spice to a somewhat bland flavor profile for a chicken dish his mentor was attempting to perfect. Here he is shown prior to preparing his first dish at the institute. However, tasters would only comment "Tastes like chicken."

Twice-removed great aunt Leda Corsica Hamblyn is shown here with her pet stork, Rockwell. We always wanted to tell her, before she passed away, that in this photo she looks like a young Betty White. We never told her because Rockwell was always there, and he didn't look like anyone we knew.

Twelve-times-removed third cousin Vladmir Januszewski (pictured with hammer) was the commander of an elite tactical squad, codenamed "The Black Hoods", who were trained to conduct operations at the sound of a hammer on steel. Sadly, the squad was wiped out in their first engagement by a marauding flock of white storks, which are also, ironically, the Polish National Bird.

Our family has a history of activism. Family members have joined movements such as Save The Alaskan Canary (STAC), Surveyors Against Maine Lobsterman and Steelworkers Union (SAMLASU), Stop Illegal Lithuanian Immigration (SILI), and Crocodiles & Reptiles Are Pets Too (CRAPT). In the photo below, six-times-removed second cousin Wilburetta Summer Slovenkin joins her sisters-in-arms in a protest march for Ban Alcohol Based Mouthwashes (BABM). She's the pretty, smiling one.

This is a very old photo, taken at the very first Thanksgiving held in New Haven, Connecticut back in, like, 1640 or whenever. Here, supposed family members enjoy a new food called chicken, introduced by the Indians, and then have a smoke.

This is fourth cousin nine-times-removed Alexander Tovarishch Samlasu. He was trusted Physician to the Imperial Court of Tsar Nicholas II, Emperor and Autocrat of All the Russias, Grand Duke of Finland, Saint Nicholas the Passion-Bearer. Or maybe he was a wizard or something.

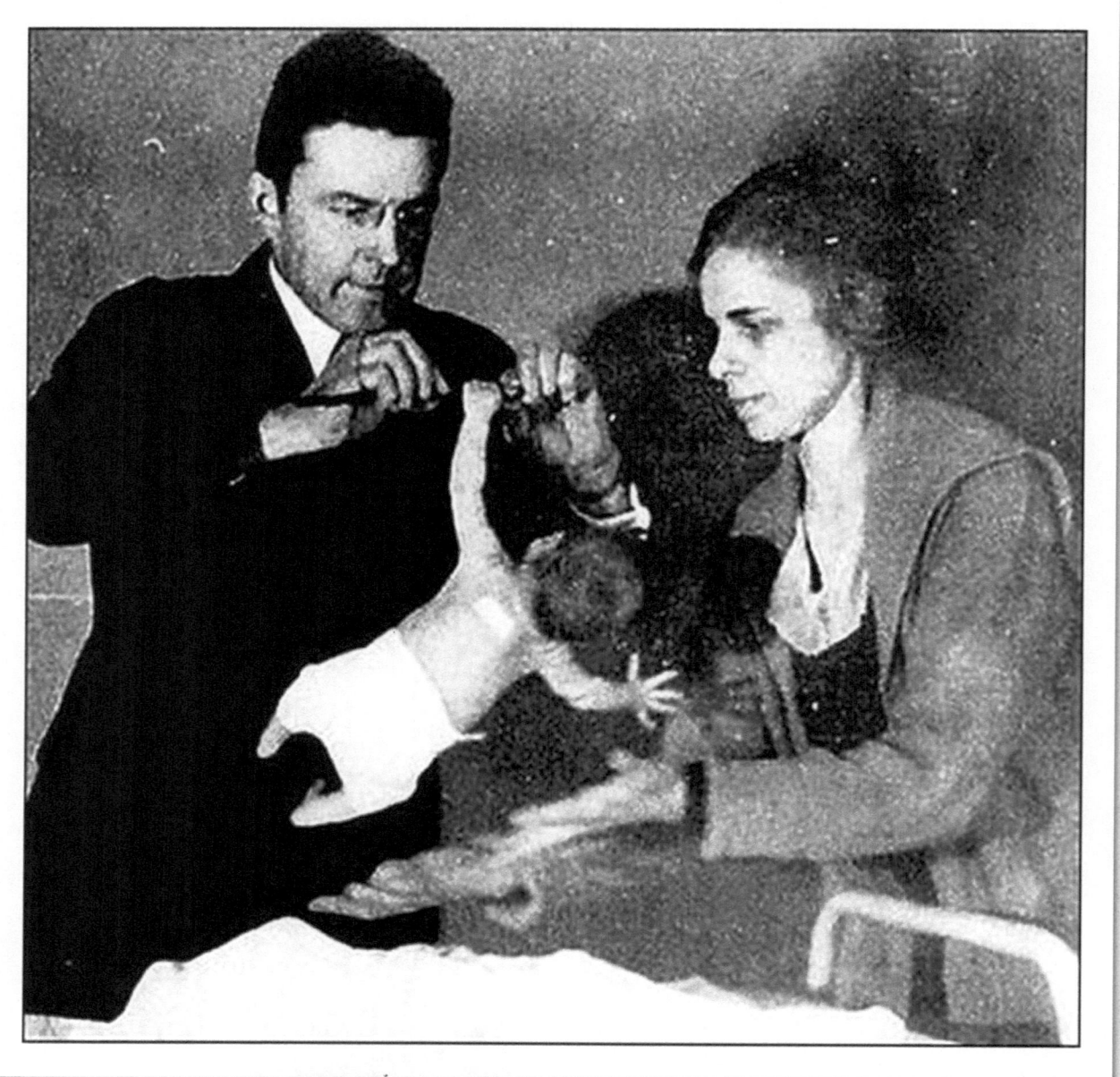

Directly after his birth, thrice-removed fourth cousin Herbert von Nuemann was recognized as The World's Strongest Baby. Here he is shown performing one-handed pull-ups assisted by Doctors Marcus Feelgood and Eloise Crachett. Little Herbert was probably most famous for pulling a fully-loaded Alaskan whaleboat three hundred feet, using only his binky.

Boxers and twin brothers, fifth cousins twice-removed Percy and Lowell Vonnegot were both heavyweight hopefuls who lacked common sense and were twisted by a cultish spirituality. Here they are shown worshipping the head of Heavyweight Champion Joe Louis, a practice they continued until their father, housepainter Walter Vonnegot, reclaimed his borrowed ladder.

Fourth cousin six-times-removed Jackson Dane Cooner was proud to serve in the American Expeditionary Force in World War I. In this photo he's preparing to dig a trench with his unit near Compiegne, France, in 1917. That's Jackson on the far right, next to the tree.

No, next to the tree.

There are no family members associated with this photo or with the animals pictured here.

I just like this photo. A lot.

In this photo Bibi Jinright, wife of nine-times-removed fourth cousin Marco Jinright, demonstrates her husband's invention, the Rodeo Boot —designed to stop women from shopping for shoes. She didn't like it. No one did.

Four-times-removed fourth cousin and intrepid pilot Barney "Barnstorm" Blaney and his faithful sidekick Butch The Wonder Dog are shown here prior to their attempted record-breaking 'round-the-world flight. The flight had to be postponed, however, in order to treat third-degree burns on Barney's back.

Twice-removed sixth cousin Jonathan Starr, marked in this photo with an "X", was lead guitarist in an early inception of the popular post-punk musical group, Echo & The Bunnymen. That's Echo, standing, with beard.

Back in 1924 five-times-removed second cousin Dixie Flaubert-Bingenheimer set out to drive coast-to-coast in this miniature car, with the American Automobile Association as her sponsor. We think she's still somewhere in Oklahoma. If you see her please call 1-800-AAA-HELP.

The family is also known for their inventiveness. Here somewhat confused third cousin five-times-removed Heloise May Birnbaum is shown demonstrating one of her two inventions, the Auto-Mechanical Hair Desiccation Device. Afterward, when all she could say was "Cluck-cluck beAACH!" it was discovered that this was, instead, her other invention—The Auto-Mechanical Brain Transfer Device. (Chicken not shown.)

Twice-removed fifth cousin Myrtle Carey Malander is shown here with her invention, the weatherproof fully-enclosed surfboard.

Eight-times-removed fourth cousin Fidel Darius Charan spent years cultivating strange and mystical abilities. It wasn't until he studied in the Indus Valley at the feet of outlaw Sufi mystic Baba Hazmat Abdul Shakarbardar that he was able to perform the feat of object levitation. He used this strange and powerful power to start a popular and successful business, Fidel's Furniture Movers, Inc.

Animal trainer and sixth-removed third cousin Cordelia Simpson Bloomhart is shown here with her highly-intelligent domestic crow, Poe. Using a reward system, Cordie was able to train Poe to light a match and use it to light her cigarette. Once Poe was trained the reward was removed. Unfortunately, two weeks later Cordie's house burnt down.

Here, brothers and fifth-removed fourth cousins Frederick and Klaus Sturmer are shown outside the Swiss cantonment of Aix-la-Chapelle demonstrating their invention, invisible stairs. Understandably, their invention never found widespread use.

An early proponent of so-called Green technology, Gutherie Cavanaugh Sharpnack, sixth cousin twice-removed, is seen here with his invention — the ultra-compact SMARTcarriage.

Alvaro Sandino Secondo, nineteen-times-removed third cousin, is shown here demonstrating his invention, the Auto-Mechanical Matter Transmission

Device. Alvaro had only enough money for one "cage" (the construct he's seated in), so this highly-successful machine was capable of transmitting matter only to itself — over and over and over and over and over.

...nth-removed
...ourth cousin
...ouis "Ché" Burgeon
...erved proudly with
...he World War II
...rench resistance
...ilitia, Les
...épugnant Monkees.

Four-times-removed fourth cousin Hubert McClintock, right, and his son Hubert McClintock, left, show off their axes.

Third cousin twice-etcetera Doyle "Cliff" Dunhill was appointed Grand Marshall of National Kick-The-Pickle Week. Here he is shown with Dora Sinclair, Women's National Kick-The Pickle Champion, preparing to kick-the-pickle.

Thaddeus Bosko Byron, world-famous explorer, botanist, and six-times-removed fourth cousin, traveled the far reaches of the Pacific Ocean to the tiny lost island group of Synamares Atoll to find this specimen, which at 630 pounds is the world's largest booger.

Eight-times removed third cousin Eloise "Sparky" Cantreau, right, models her invention, the glass face-cone. Intended to prevent bug hits during the brand-new activity of automobile touring, her efforts were negated by another invention, the windshield.

Trend-setting five-times-removed sixth cousins Mercy, Patience, and Lothar Portney are shown here in a recreation of the moment they invented "Playing Doctor." They were never able to patent their invention, though, and thus received no royalties.

Conjoined twins Henrick and Davis Plotbotham-Curlice, twelfth cousins twice-removed, are here shown strolling the concourse at Ascot Raceway directly before the running of the 1911 Derby.

In this photo thrice-removed eighth cousin Henri Pertoussain is shown with his French Air Force flight group during WWI, testing a new bomb-delivery method.

Thomasina Corbutt, fifth cousin three times removed, was 1933 Short Track Griddle-Skating World Champion. She is shown here with her trophy, a giant plywood spatula.

Little Ricky Timmons Perceival III, twice-removed ninth cousin, really loved bird cages. And hated oversized hair bows.

Tenth cousin twice-removed Takira Tamasaka is shown here in his role as stand-in for Godzilla during the monster's infamous destruction of Tokyo in 1954. In 1973 Takira was promoted to Megalon, and joined Godzilla in destroying Tokyo once again.

Sixth cousin ninth-times-removed Chloe K. Chamberlain was a successful dancer and designer who succumbed to alcoholism after her design for the CBS "eye" logo was rejected.

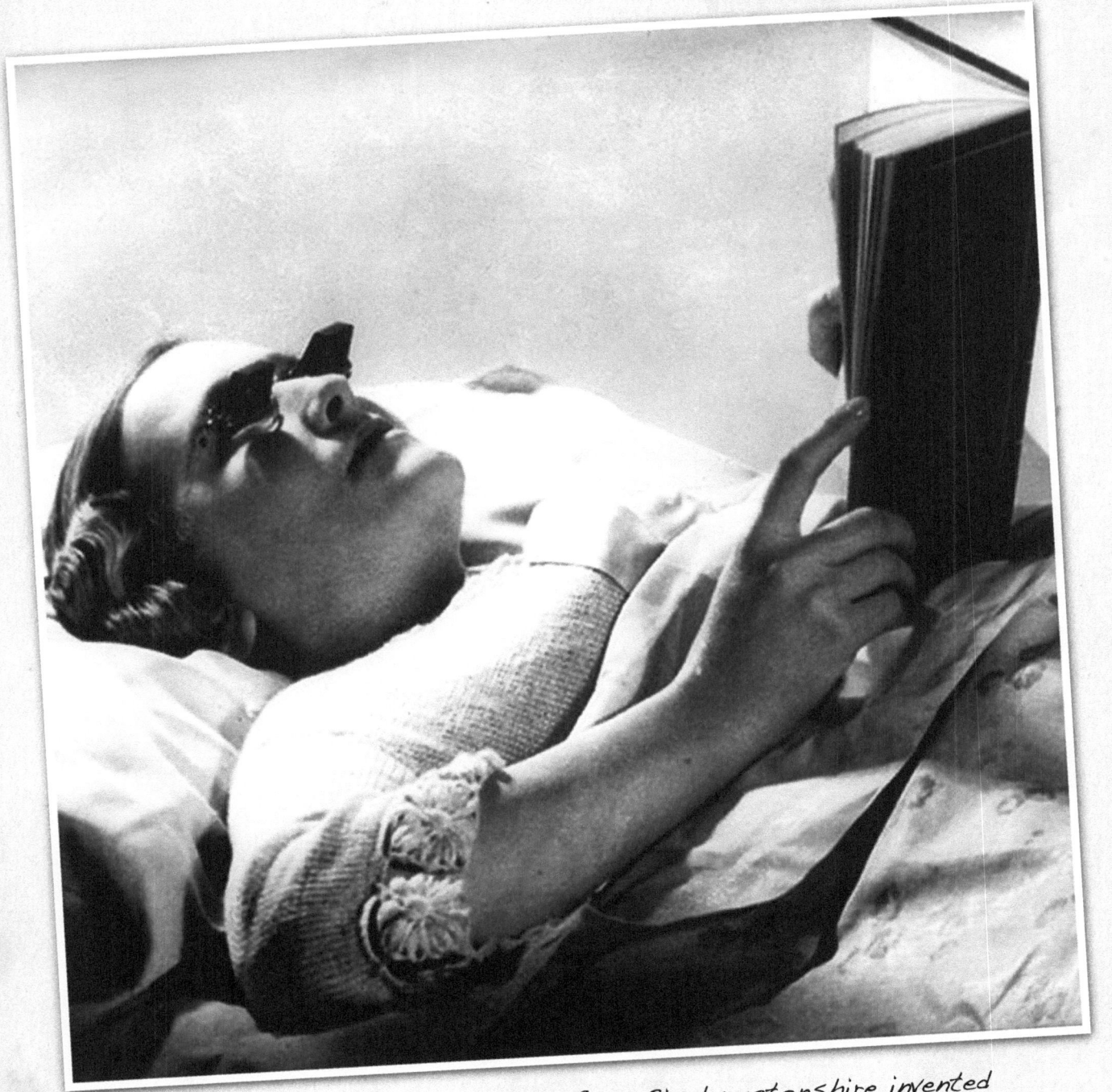

Eleventh cousin twice-removed Rose Binghamptonshire invented prismatic glasses which allowed a person to read while prone in bed. Members of the family are very ingenious. And lazy.

In this photo, eleventh cousin twice-removed Rose Binghamptonshire is shown with an invention which enabled her to give organ recitals while

sleeping. Later, she combined this invention with the prismatic glasses (see previous photo) which gave her the ability to play while dreaming in primary colours.

The group mistakenly believed ninth-removed second cousin Kate Kernshaw would behave in a more adult-like manner when they refused to let her play "Choo-Choo" with them.

Twice-removed fourth cousin Conrad Blythe-Davis used his many heads to impress the ladies.

Early mythbuster Earl Tarkentonton, relation unknown, here attempts to disprove another old wives tale by dressing in wolves clothing. His confusion led to several gunshot wounds.

Four-times-removed fifth cousin
Clarice Lee Norbit, an early and innovative automotive designer, is shown here driving her creation "The Tisket." Clarice's efforts to market the wicker automobile to egg ranchers failed miserably.

Kaspar "Kap" Mann considered himself to be a super-hero on the ski slopes above Innsbruck, Austria, but in reality he scared more people than he saved. Fourth cousin six-times-removed, he spent the off-season on the French Riviera working as a pissed-off mime.

Four-times-removed third cousin Annabelle McCauley discovered, accidentally, that her rooftop sharpshooting skills increased if she wore only her underwear. In this photo, Wiggins the Wonder Dog gazes on her in Wonder.

Seven-times-removed seventh cousin Gaston "Friedo" Fredette was disowned by The Family for reasons other than being a horrible mime and a Frenchman. Cousin Friedo, you are dead to us!

Fifth cousin twice-removed Betty Jo Caruso was voted Miss Unknown Beauty in 1939. That's her, second from the left... or is she second from the right? Hell, I don't know...

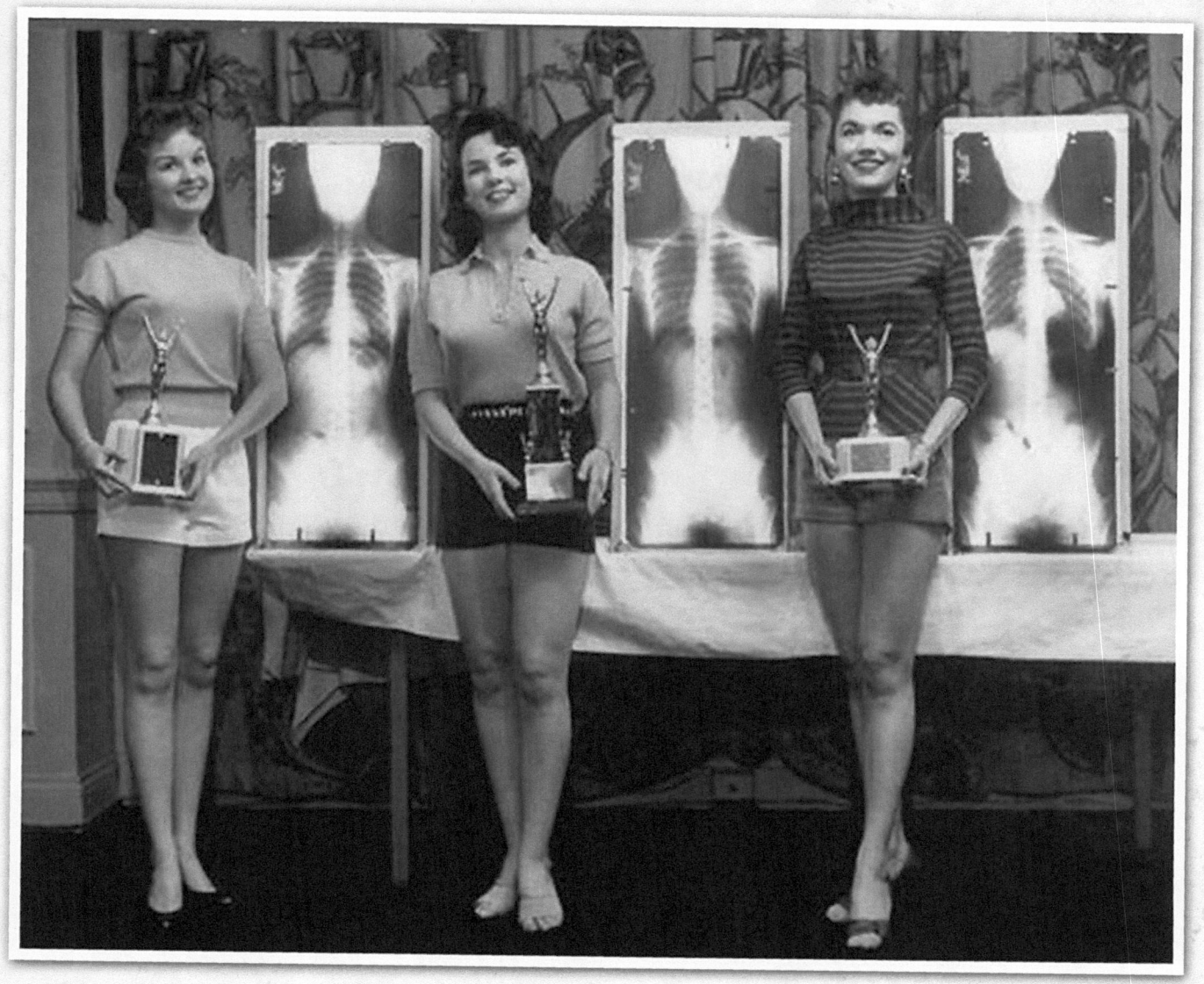

Five-times-removed ninth cousin
Cynthia Ann Mayer, center, is shown here holding her first-place Miss
Beautiful Skeleton trophy in 1954. She competed regularly in the contest
until 1958, when she was forced to drop out due to radiation poisoning.

Edna Mae Larsen, far left and fourth cousin five-times-removed, was owner and proprietor of Big Chief Root Beer, alongside Route 66 near Clearwater, Oklahoma. The business soon went bust, but Edna never could understand why people were reluctant to buy root beer from the gaping mouth of a giant pissed-off Indian head.

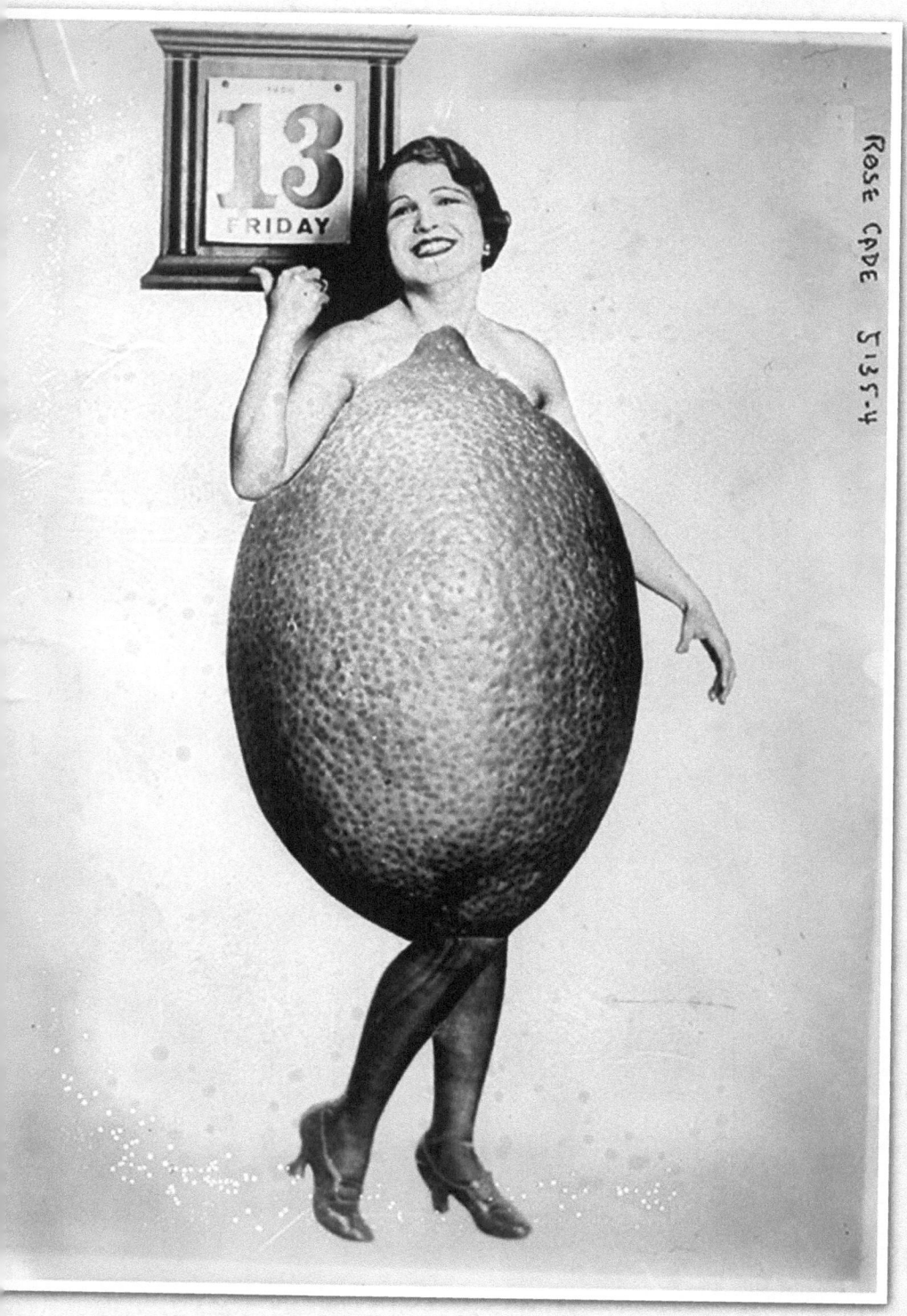

Seventh-removed fourth cousin Rose Sampson Cade was the inaugural Miss Lemon for the Lemon Festival in Upland, California. However, she was extremely superstitious and so failed to show up for the crowning ceremony.

Sixth cousin fourth-removed Aleksandr "Sasha" Balakleets, a farmer in the Ukraine, had very poor eyesight.

Tenth cousin thrice-removed Herbert Cainlin and his wife Eloise were, unfortunately, unable to have children despite their best efforts. Later in life they became activists in the fertility movement. Here they are shown at the National Fertility Foundation's Memorial Garden at Baltimore, Maryland in 1938.

As a child, Mercy Tingle (fourth cousin seven-times-removed) absolutely loved camels. She grew out of it.

Grigory Fedor Alexey, ninth cousin, was chosen to be the first infant cosmonaut by the Russian Federal Space Agency. His flight was scrubbed at the last minute due to poorly-designed space-nappies.

Conjoined twins and thrice-removed ninth cousins Doris and Leticia Sinclair are shown here relaxing in the back yard of their home at Inbred, Ohio.

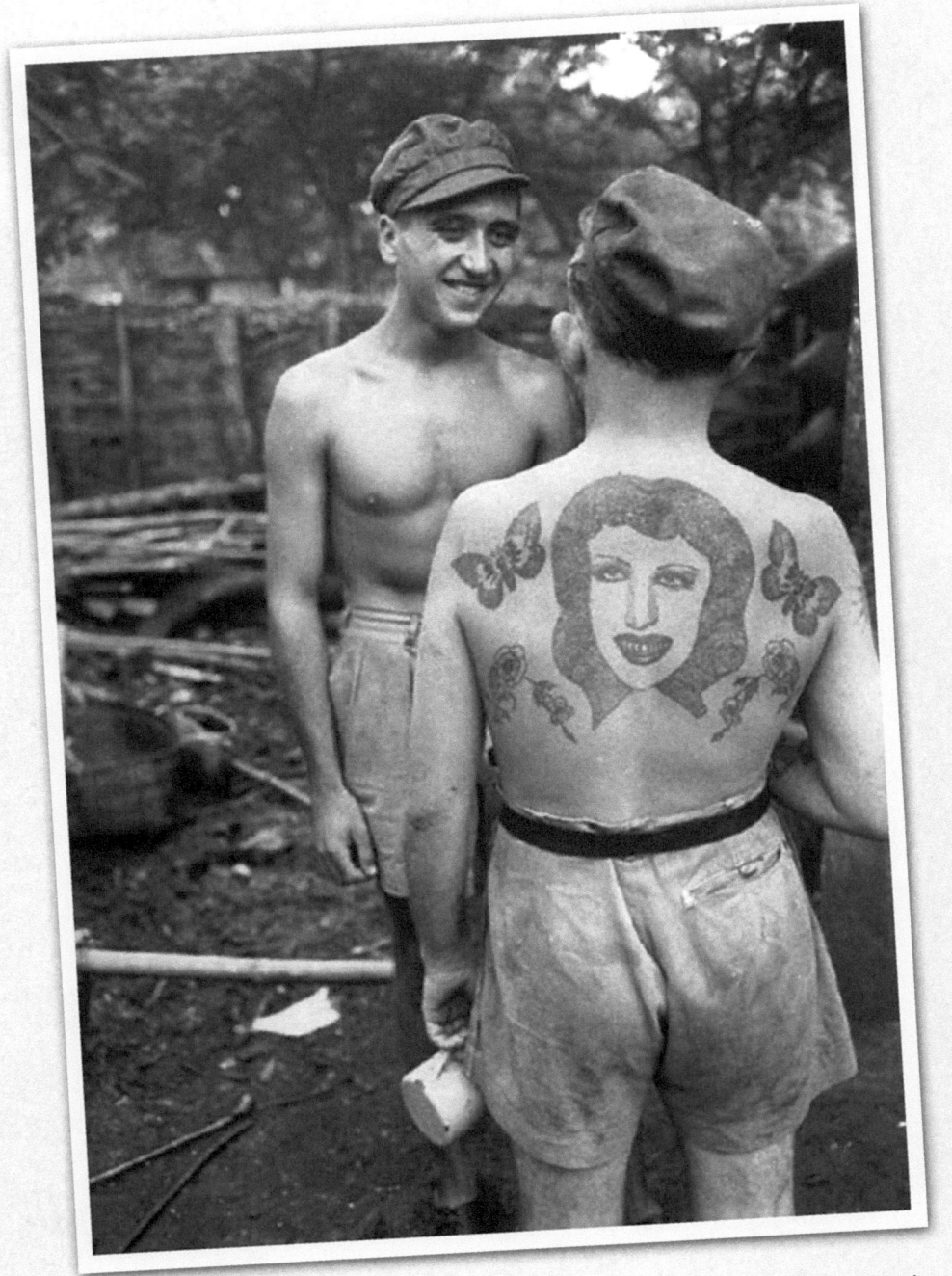

Aspiring tattoo artist and third cousin fifth-removed Harvey Tilden Beliot, facing, accepts payment and thanks from fellow soldier Gus Perkins after successfully completing a life-size rendition of Gus' lovely girlfriend, Hilda.

Seventh cousin Robert "Bob" Kinsman and his family were often accused of having a dinosaur.

From a young age,
eleventh cousin twice-removed Johann "Jonny"
Gresfelt was quite the ladies man.

Third cousin five-times-removed Gus 'Pinkeye' Flussnatch, center top, is shown here shortly after his invention of "I'm With Stupid." Wild times.

Sixth cousin four-times-removed Harry "Weather" Loudon was very serious about his lifelong career in the Child Delivery Corps.

During the Great Depression, fourth cousin three-times-removed Thomas Maynard Pincalde was forced by circumstance to work as a bumper.

Here seventh cousin Harry Simms, a mannequin salesman, is seen showing his wares at a mannequin swap meet held at Black Rock Desert, Nevada, in 1944. Harry went on to become a successful mannequin manufacturer but was forced to close his business when the market was flooded by cheaper and more durable Chinese-made asbestos mannequins. That's Harry holding the hammer.

Twelfth cousins thrice-removed Theresa and Johnson Bartlett were active nudists. Here they are shown arriving with a friend at Olympic Fields Nudist Camp in 1923, unaware that it had closed.

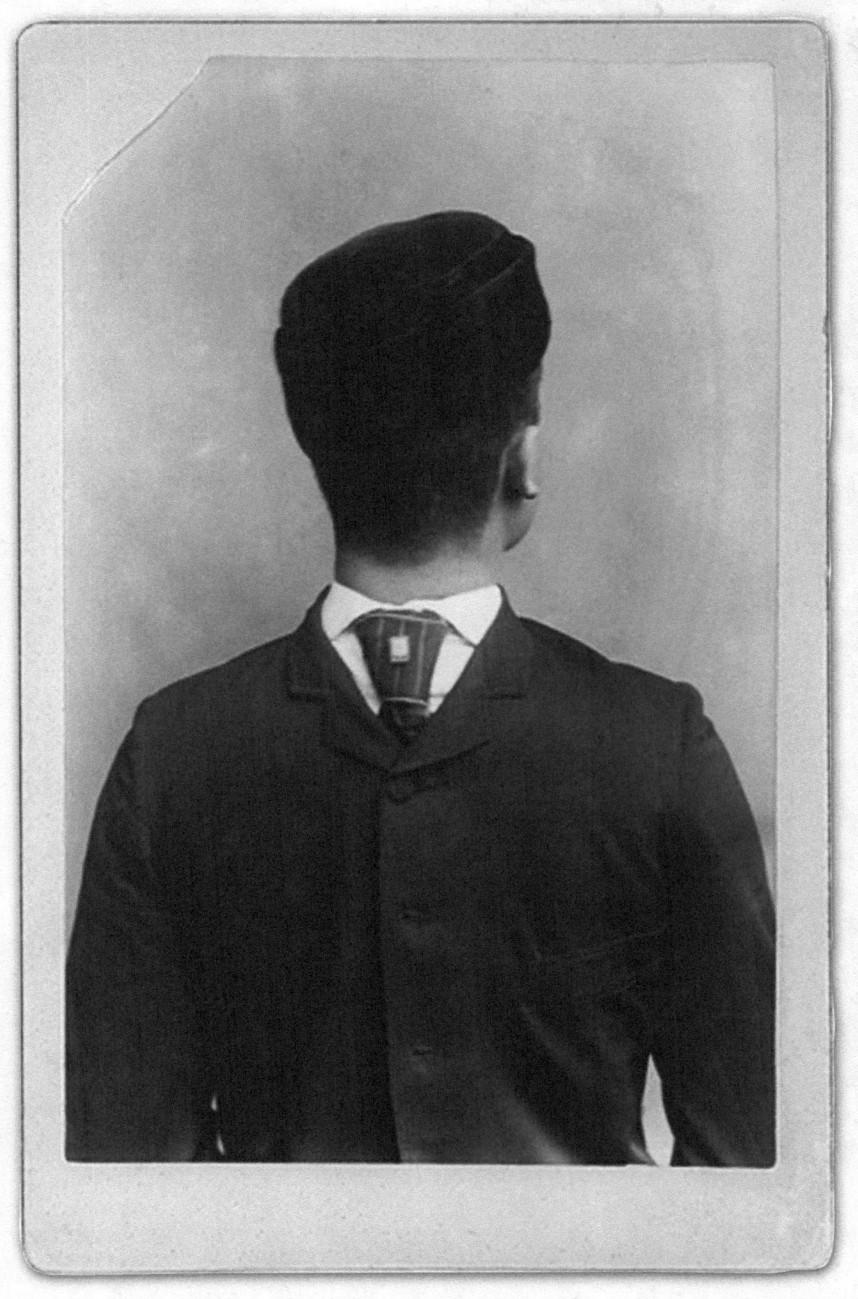

Fifth-removed eighth cousin Christopher Bohannon was born with a minor congenital defect. Or he had problems dressing, I forget.

Jameson Reis, eighth-removed fourth cousin, was the inventor and sole patent-holder of this, the human-powered vacuum.

This is tenth cousin twice-removed Gordon Tatum-Pierce.
He was quite large and, well, very good at picking up women.

The Author in Fancy Dress as a Side of Bacon, designed by himself, which took the First Prize of Forty Guineas at the Covent Garden Fancy Dress Ball, April 1894.

Sixth cousin twice-removed Kayden Briar Kemp won first prize by dressing as a side of bacon. His wife Bella, not shown, was costumed even more spectacularly as an egg, but was unable to attend due to an unfortunate "cracking" incident.

Twelfth cousin Edna "Granny" Smith was an early practitioner of parkour, or "free-running." However, due to her advanced age she needed help overcoming most urban obstacles.

Seventh-removed fourth cousin Dorthea Spillburton Tang was, at different times, the winner of both the "Miss Chicken" and the "Miss Egg" pageants —the first in 1898 and the second in 1897.

Or was it the other way around?

Sixth cousin thrice-removed Delbert Flournoy Delvechio was under the mistaken impression that his "magical" hard hat and overalls made him invisible to humans. He successfully practiced the effect for years, on rooms full of fake people.

Missy LaTouche Peterson, fifth cousin four-times removed, loved to play "Surprise!" with her husband while they both wore masks.

We thought it was creepy, too.

www.ingramcontent.com/pod-product-compliance
Lightning Source LLC
Chambersburg PA
CBHW060818090426
42738CB00002B/32